THE #HOLYMISCHIEF LENTEN CHALLENGE

A DEVOTIONAL AND GUIDE TO PRACTICING ACTS OF KINDNESS DURING LENT.

REV DR SHANNON E KARAFANDA

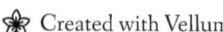 Created with Vellum

This book is dedicated to:

Rev. Scott Parrish's goats. Thanks to your owner for connecting me to the term #HolyMischief. Thanks for popping in a few Zoom calls during the Pandemic. Thanks for keeping social media posts fresh, fun, and cute! Oh and please don't eat any paper copies of this book. Thanks again!

-Rev. Dr. Shannon E. Karafanda

Thank you.

[No. Really. Thanks!]

Thanks for joining us in the Holy Mischief Lenten Challenge!

Lent is a season of time that can lead us into more disciplined, focused lives...the period of 40 days leading up to Easter (*note: Sundays don't count*). It is a time of preparation and focus. It is designed to help us become the people God has created and called us to be.

What kind of person is that? One who engages in the mysterious and divine disruptions of life by putting God's love in action.

Over the next 40 days, we will go on a journey together learning about the holy mischief Jesus engaged in, praying about where God is calling us, and challenging ourselves to put that call into action.

Each day you'll be encouraged to pick a challenge, read from the Gospels, and discover things that Jesus did that broke the script of everyday life. You can go in order and do a different challenge each day or pick and choose a challenge based on interest and availability.

The focus should be doing something that share's God's love. Sometimes the challenges will be easy; while other times you'll need to stretch yourself, but with the right mindset, it will certainly be joyful and can change the world.

Thanks again!
Happy Holy Mischiefing,
Rev. Dr. Shannon E. Karafanda

P.S. – For some extra inspiration, join us on the Facebook group: facebook.com/groups/holymischiefmakers

We'd love for you to share stories of your adventures with the group!

40 CHALLENGES OF #HOLYMISCHIEF

#HOLYMISCHIEF
LENTEN CHALLENGE

1. Fast.
2. Give someone directions.
3. Ask someone to join you in a challenge.
4. Write a note to a spiritual mentor.
5. Use only positive words today.
6. Offer water to a guest and get their story.
7. Visit someone who is sick or deliver a gift to a nurses' station.
8. Eat with someone you wouldn't normally eat with.
9. Pray for your enemy.
10. Give a "light" to someone in a service job.
11. Call someone who is like a brother or sister to you.
12. Donate fresh fruit to a local food pantry.
13. Pray the Lord's Prayer twice today. Alone and then with another believer.
14. Share with your family how you think the world could better.
15. Rainy day? Share your umbrella with someone walking through a parking lot.

1

16. Give a mint to someone.

17. Surprise someone with a celebration just because they are awesome!

18. Share something you know to be true with someone else.

19. Pay it backwards.

20. Donate or volunteer your time in children's ministry or a local school.

21. Post inspirational sticky notes around your neighborhood, office, school etc.

22. Smile at five strangers today.

23. Remove things in your life that might tempt you. Ask someone to hold you accountable.

24. Pray for your city. Invite a friend to go on a prayer walk with you.

25. Give up your cell phones during a meal today and talk about the scripture with someone.

26. Have a "mini-parade" for anyone who walks through your door/ cubicle today.

27. Give a stranger $20 today. Share their reaction.

28. Deliver fresh baked bread to the local fire or police station.

29. Send someone a "ewe" with a nice note in the mail.

30. Practice Lectio Divina with the scripture today.

31. Wash windows or clean the toilets of a local business today.

32. Invite someone to a Holy Week service.

33. Hug someone and tell them you love them.

34. Write down all the names of Jesus that you can think of.

35. Put a note at your table or desk asking how you can pray for others.

36. Pray for the leaders of your city or state today. Send them a note telling them you did.
37. Tell others about your faith.
38. Go one day without social media and television.
39. Pray today at 9:00 am, 12:00 pm, and 3:00 pm.
40. Spend one day without talking.

CHALLENGE #1
FAST

#HOLYMISCHIEF
LENTEN CHALLENGE

Your challenge: Prepare to fast. Pick a meal (an activity if fasting would be detrimental to your health) to give up in the next day or so. During that time pray and listen to God. Where is he calling you to share His love? What can you do with the money you would've spent on that meal or made during that time you were praying?

MATTHEW 4:1-11

> **4** Then Jesus was led up by the Spirit into the wilderness to be tempted by the devil. **2** He fasted forty days and forty nights, and afterwards he was famished. **3** The tempter came and said to him, "If you are the Son of God, command these stones to become loaves of bread." **4** But he answered, "It is written,

'One does not live by bread alone,
    but by every word that comes from the
        mouth of God.'"

5 Then the devil took him to the holy city and
    placed him on the pinnacle of the
    temple, *6* saying to him, "If you are the Son
    of God, throw yourself down; for it is
    written,

'He will command his angels concerning you,'
    and 'On their hands they will bear you up,
so that you will not dash your foot against a
    stone.'"

7 Jesus said to him, "Again it is written, 'Do
    not put the Lord your God to the test.'"

8 Again, the devil took him to a very high
    mountain and showed him all the king-
    doms of the world and their
    splendor; *9* and he said to him, "All these I
    will give you, if you will fall down and
    worship me." *10* Jesus said to him, "Away
    with you, Satan! for it is written,

'Worship the Lord your God,
    and serve only him.'"

11 Then the devil left him, and suddenly
    angels came and waited on him.

There is a strong biblical base for fasting, particularly during the 40 days of Lent leading to the celebration of Easter. Fasting has been a part of Methodism from its early beginnings. John Wesley considered fasting an important part of a

Christian's life and he fasted weekly. To Wesley, fasting was an important way to express sorrow for sin and penitence for overindulgence in eating and drinking. He believed it allowed more time for prayer and was more meaningful if combined with giving to the poor. Wesley did advise caution against extreme fasting and against fasting for those in fragile health.

CHALLENGE #2
GIVE SOMEONE DIRECTIONS

Your challenge: People are rarely lost anymore. GPS apps and cell phones have made life much easier. But sometimes we don't know what we're looking for. We don't always know the best restaurant, doctor, or store to go to. Recommend a local business to someone else today. It might come in handy for them at some point and it will do a lot for the local business in your community.

LUKE 2:41-52

> **41** *Now every year his parents went to Jerusalem for the festival of the Passover.* **42** *And when he was twelve years old, they went up as usual for the festival.* **43** *When the festival was ended and they started to return, the boy Jesus*

*stayed behind in Jerusalem, but his parents did not know it. **44** Assuming that he was in the group of travelers, they went a day's journey. Then they started to look for him among their relatives and friends. **45** When they did not find him, they returned to Jerusalem to search for him. **46** After three days they found him in the temple, sitting among the teachers, listening to them and asking them questions. **47** And all who heard him were amazed at his understanding and his answers. **48** When his parents saw him they were astonished; and his mother said to him, "Child, why have you treated us like this? Look, your father and I have been searching for you in great anxiety." **49** He said to them, "Why were you searching for me? Did you not know that I must be in my Father's house?" **50** But they did not understand what he said to them. **51** Then he went down with them and came to Nazareth, and was obedient to them. His mother treasured all these things in her heart.*

52 *And Jesus increased in wisdom and in years, and in divine and human favor.*

We often think that someone who is lost is the one experiencing worry or anxiety when often it is the person searching for what is lost. People without faith don't know they are lost. They can't know what they are missing out on if they've never had it. Show them the beauty of faith. Once they figure out that you have something worth looking for, they'll ask for directions.

———————

CHALLENGE #3
ASK SOMEONE TO JOIN YOU IN A CHALLENGE

#HOLYMISCHIEF
LENTEN CHALLENGE

Your challenge: Who can you ask to go on a Holy Mischief adventure together? Pray about it and then reach out to them. Ask them to join you in a challenge this week. Invite them to join you for all of Lent and add them to the Facebook group.

JOHN 1:35-51

The First Disciples of Jesus

35 The next day John again was standing with two of his disciples, 36 and as he watched Jesus walk by, he exclaimed, "Look, here is the Lamb of God!" 37 The two disciples heard him say this, and they followed Jesus. 38 When Jesus turned and saw them following, he said to them, "What are you looking for?" They said to him,

13

"Rabbi" (which translated means Teacher), "where are you staying?" **39** He said to them, "Come and see." They came and saw where he was staying, and they remained with him that day. It was about four o'clock in the afternoon. **40** One of the two who heard John speak and followed him was Andrew, Simon Peter's brother. **41** He first found his brother Simon and said to him, "We have found the Messiah" (which is translated Anointed). **42** He brought Simon to Jesus, who looked at him and said, "You are Simon son of John. You are to be called Cephas" (which is translated Peter).

Jesus Calls Philip and Nathanael

43 The next day Jesus decided to go to Galilee. He found Philip and said to him, "Follow me." **44** Now Philip was from Bethsaida, the city of Andrew and Peter. **45** Philip found Nathanael and said to him, "We have found him about whom Moses in the law and also the prophets wrote, Jesus son of Joseph from Nazareth." **46** Nathanael said to him, "Can anything good come out of Nazareth?" Philip said to him, "Come and see." **47** When Jesus saw Nathanael coming toward him, he said of him, "Here is truly an Israelite in whom there is no deceit!" **48** Nathanael asked him, "Where did you get to know me?" Jesus answered, "I saw you under the fig tree before Philip

called you." **49** Nathanael replied, "Rabbi,
you are the Son of God! You are the King of
Israel!" **50** Jesus answered, "Do you
believe because I told you that I saw you
under the fig tree? You will see greater
things than these." **51** And he said to him,
"Very truly, I tell you, you will see heaven
opened and the angels of God ascending
and descending upon the Son of Man."

———

Following Jesus changes us. Following Jesus together changes
the world. Find ways to change the world as often as you can.

———

CHALLENGE #4
WRITE A NOTE TO A SPIRITUAL MENTOR

Your challenge: Pray about who has been an influence in your life in your decision to follow Jesus. Email, text, call, visit, or write this person thanking them for their role in your life. If you are unable to connect with them for some reason, write about them and tell someone else what they meant to you.

LUKE 4:16 -30

> *16 When he came to Nazareth, where he had been brought up, he went to the synagogue on the sabbath day, as was his custom. He stood up to read, 17 and the scroll of the prophet Isaiah was given to him. He unrolled the scroll and found the place where it was written:*

18

"The Spirit of the Lord is upon me,
   because he has anointed me
     to bring good news to the poor.
He has sent me to proclaim release to the
     captives
   and recovery of sight to the blind,
     to let the oppressed go free,
19 *to proclaim the year of the Lord's favor."*

20 *And he rolled up the scroll, gave it back to the attendant, and sat down. The eyes of all in the synagogue were fixed on him.* **21** *Then he began to say to them, "Today this scripture has been fulfilled in your hearing."* **22** *All spoke well of him and were amazed at the gracious words that came from his mouth. They said, "Is not this Joseph's son?"* **23** *He said to them, "Doubtless you will quote to me this proverb, 'Doctor, cure yourself!' And you will say, 'Do here also in your hometown the things that we have heard you did at Capernaum.'"* **24** *And he said, "Truly I tell you, no prophet is accepted in the prophet's hometown.* **25** *But the truth is, there were many widows in Israel in the time of Elijah, when the heaven was shut up three years and six months, and there was a severe famine over all the land;* **26** *yet Elijah was sent to none of them except to a widow at Zarephath in*

*Sidon. **27** There were also many lepers in Israel in the time of the prophet Elisha, and none of them was cleansed except Naaman the Syrian." **28** When they heard this, all in the synagogue were filled with rage. **29** They got up, drove him out of the town, and led him to the brow of the hill on which their town was built, so that they might hurl him off the cliff. **30** But he passed through the midst of them and went on his way.*

Once we follow Jesus, people treat us differently. Some are excited for us; some are in shock. Many are watching how are lives are transforming. We usually don't come to the decision to follow Jesus without other influences in our lives.

CHALLENGE #5
USE ONLY POSITIVE WORDS TODAY

#HOLYMISCHIEF

Your challenge: Be positive with your words today. Say positive things to yourself and others.

MATTHEW 5:1-12

The Beatitudes

5 When Jesus saw the crowds, he went up the mountain; and after he sat down, his disciples came to him. 2 Then he began to speak, and taught them, saying:

3 "Blessed are the poor in spirit, for theirs is the kingdom of heaven.

4 "Blessed are those who mourn, for they will be comforted.

5 "Blessed are the meek, for they will inherit the earth.

6 *"Blessed are those who hunger and thirst for righteousness, for they will be filled.*

7 *"Blessed are the merciful, for they will receive mercy.*

8 *"Blessed are the pure in heart, for they will see God.*

9 *"Blessed are the peacemakers, for they will be called children of God.*

10 *"Blessed are those who are persecuted for righteousness' sake, for theirs is the kingdom of heaven.*

11 *"Blessed are you when people revile you and persecute you and utter all kinds of evil against you falsely on my account.* **12** *Rejoice and be glad, for your reward is great in heaven, for in the same way they persecuted the prophets who were before you.*

Happiness comes in many ways. As followers of Jesus, we find happiness in ways that might challenge others, but when others see us full of joy, even when things don't go our way, they wonder why.

CHALLENGE #6

OFFER WATER TO A GUEST AND GET THEIR STORY

#HOLYMISCHIEF
LENTEN CHALLENGE

Your challenge: Buy bottled water or an extra water bottle, and keep it at your desk, home, in your backpack. It needs to be somewhere that will be easy for you to share it with others. Offer water to those who visit your office, home, or that you meet somewhere new. Ask them to tell you their story. Watch God at work.

JOHN 2:1-12

The Wedding at Cana

> **2** On the third day there was a wedding in Cana of Galilee, and the mother of Jesus was there. **2** Jesus and his disciples had also been invited to the wedding. **3** When the wine gave out, the mother of Jesus said to him, "They have no wine." **4** And Jesus

said to her, "Woman, what concern is that to you and to me? My hour has not yet come." **5** His mother said to the servants, "Do whatever he tells you." **6** Now standing there were six stone water jars for the Jewish rites of purification, each holding twenty or thirty gallons. **7** Jesus said to them, "Fill the jars with water." And they filled them up to the brim. **8** He said to them, "Now draw some out, and take it to the chief steward." So they took it. **9** When the steward tasted the water that had become wine, and did not know where it came from (though the servants who had drawn the water knew), the steward called the bridegroom **10** and said to him, "Everyone serves the good wine first, and then the inferior wine after the guests have become drunk. But you have kept the good wine until now." **11** Jesus did this, the first of his signs, in Cana of Galilee, and revealed his glory; and his disciples believed in him.

12 After this he went down to Capernaum with his mother, his brothers, and his disciples; and they remained there a few days.

Jesus is the bringer of God's overflowing grace. Everyone has a story that shows how God has been at work in their lives.

They may not know how God has shown up, but by hearing someone else's story, you're inviting them into a more intimate relationship with both you and God.

———

CHALLENGE #7

VISIT SOMEONE WHO IS SICK OR DELIVER A
GIFT TO A NURSES' STATION

Your challenge: Visit someone who is sick and if you don't know someone who is sick, bring a treat (mints, flowers, candy etc) to a doctor's office or nurses' station as they care for those who are sick.

MARK 2:1-12

Jesus Heals a Paralytic

2 When he returned to Capernaum after some days, it was reported that he was at home. 2 So many gathered around that there was no longer room for them, not even in front of the door; and he was speaking the word to them. 3 Then some people came, bringing to him a paralyzed man, carried by four of them. 4 And when they could not bring him to Jesus because of the crowd, they removed the roof above him; and after having dug through it, they let down the mat on which the paralytic lay. *5* When Jesus saw their faith, he said to the paralytic, "Son, your sins are forgiven." *6* Now some of the scribes were sitting there, questioning in their hearts, *7* "Why does this fellow speak in this way? It is blasphemy! Who can forgive sins but God alone?" *8* At once Jesus perceived in his spirit that they were discussing these questions among themselves; and he said to them, "Why do you raise such questions in your hearts? *9* Which is easier, to say to the paralytic, 'Your sins are forgiven,' or to say, 'Stand up and take your mat and walk'? *10* But so that you may know that the Son of Man has authority on earth to forgive sins"—he said to the paralytic — *11* "I say to you, stand up, take your mat and go to your home." *12* And he stood up, and immediately took the mat and went out before all of them; so that they were all amazed and glorified God, saying, "We have never seen anything like this!"

Usually when we're sick, we're in no position to be around other people. However, if you stay in that state of mind for too long, you begin to lose touch with the rest of humanity. While connectivity via TV, Radio, Facebook, texting, etc all help to keep us connected during illness, there are some who are so ill that even these don't help. Electronic devices are not a substitute for a human being.

This is why visiting someone who is sick is important. This is one of those means of grace that we don't do for us; we do this for others. Sick people need to hear from you, their families need a break, and their nurses and doctors need to know that their patient isn't just another chart. I urge you to go out and visit! God will be there in your visit and you will probably learn something too.

CHALLENGE #8

EAT WITH SOMEONE YOU WOULDN'T NORMALLY EAT WITH

Your challenge: Invite someone to lunch or dinner that you don't know very well. Bonus points if you need to reconcile with this person.

LUKE 5:27-32

Jesus Calls Levi

27 *After this he went out and saw a tax collector named Levi, sitting at the tax booth; and he said to him, "Follow me."* **28** *And he got up, left everything, and followed him.*

29 *Then Levi gave a great banquet for him in his house; and there was a large crowd of tax collectors and others sitting at the table with them.* **30** *The Pharisees and their scribes were complaining to his disci-*

ples, saying, "Why do you eat and drink with tax collectors and sinners?" **31** *Jesus answered, "Those who are well have no need of a physician, but those who are sick;* **32** *I have come to call not the righteous but sinners to repentance."*

Whenever you read about a meal in the Bible, it is a signal for reconciliation. When Jesus ate with tax collectors and sinners, this was a signal that Jesus wanted everyone to be in a relationship with God. By extending an invitation to another, we are extending the love of God.

CHALLENGE #9

PRAY FOR YOUR ENEMY

Your challenge: It's easy to pray for those you love, but harder to pray for those you don't. The more we pray for our enemies, we begin to see them less like an enemy and more like a neighbor.

MATTHEW 5:45-48

> **45** *so that you may be children of your Father in heaven; for he makes his sun rise on the evil and on the good, and sends rain on the righteous and on the unrighteous.* **46** *For if you love those who love you, what reward do you have? Do not even the tax collectors do the same?* **47** *And if you greet only your brothers and sisters, what more are you doing than others? Do not even the*

Gentiles do the same? **48** *Be perfect, there-*
fore, as your heavenly Father is perfect.

As followers of Christ, we are called to love our enemies. We are to care for, pray for, provide for, and hope the best for everyone. We are not called to wish ill upon anyone, including our enemies. This radical love, agape love, is hard! It requires action, not just a general sense of goodwill or affection. How can we do it? It can only be done by the grace of God and the power of the Holy Spirit.

CHALLENGE #10

GIVE A "LIGHT" TO SOMEONE IN A SERVICE JOB

#HOLYMISCHIEF
LENTEN CHALLENGE

Your challenge: Give a flashlight, candle, glow stick or another form of light to someone who works with customers all day. Tell them how appreciative you are of their work and that the "light" you give them is a reminder that their light shines for all to see. If you don't have a "light" to give to someone, share encouraging words.

JOHN 3:1-21

Nicodemus Visits Jesus

3 Now there was a Pharisee named Nicodemus, a leader of the Jews. 2 He came to Jesus by night and said to him, "Rabbi, we know that you are a teacher who has come from God; for no one can do these signs that you do apart from the presence of God." 3 Jesus answered him, "Very truly, I tell you, no one can see the kingdom of God without being born from above." **4** Nicodemus said to him, "How can anyone be born after having grown old? Can one enter a second time into the mother's womb and be born?" **5** Jesus answered, "Very truly, I tell you, no one can enter the kingdom of God without being born of water and Spirit. **6** What is born of the flesh is flesh, and what is born of the Spirit is spirit. **7** Do not be astonished that I said to you, 'You must be born from above.' **8** The wind blows where it chooses, and you hear the sound of it, but you do not know where it comes from or where it goes. So it is with everyone who is born of the Spirit." **9** Nicodemus said to him, "How can these things be?" **10** Jesus answered him, "Are you a teacher of Israel, and yet you do not understand these things?

11 "Very truly, I tell you, we speak of what we know and testify to what we have seen; yet you do not receive our testimony. **12** If I have told you about earthly things and you do not believe, how can you believe if I tell you about heavenly things? **13** No one has ascended into heaven except the one who descended from heaven, the Son of Man. **14** And just as Moses lifted up the serpent in the wilderness, so must the Son of Man be lifted up, **15** that whoever believes in him may have eternal life.

16 "For God so loved the world that he gave his only Son, so that everyone who believes in him may not perish but may have eternal life.

17 "Indeed, God did not send the Son into the world to condemn the world, but in order that the world might be saved through him. **18** Those who believe in him are not condemned; but those who do not believe are condemned already, because they have not believed in the name of the only Son of God. **19** And this is the judgment, that the light has come into the world, and people loved darkness rather than light because their deeds were evil. **20** For all who do evil hate the light and do not come to the light, so that their deeds may not be exposed. **21** But those who do what is true come to the light, so that it may be clearly seen that their deeds have been done in God."

John Wesley said, "someone who does what is true comes to the light so that his or her deeds may be manifest in God." According to Wesley, when we practice truth, we encounter Jesus who is the light. So even Nicodemus, did what is, in the light, power, and love of God.

CHALLENGE #11

CALL SOMEONE WHO IS LIKE A BROTHER OR SISTER TO YOU

#HOLYMISCHIEF
CENTER CHALLENGE

Your challenge: Some of us are born with siblings, but most of us have a friend in our life who is like family. Call one of those people today and let them know how much they mean to you.

MARK 3:31-35

The True Kindred of Jesus

31 *Then his mother and his brothers came; and standing outside, they sent to him and called him.* **32** *A crowd was sitting around him; and they said to him, "Your mother and your brothers and sisters are outside, asking for you."* **33** *And he replied, "Who are my mother and my brothers?"* **34** *And looking at those who sat around him, he said, "Here are my mother and my broth-*

ers! **35** *Whoever does the will of God is my brother and sister and mother."*

In one of Bishop Will Willimon's sermons he says, "The gospels tell the story that the chief focus of Jesus' mission was to reconstitute the scattered lost sheep of Israel. Jesus left his biological family in order to form a new family based not on genetic kinship--that is, the way we make family--but rather upon the gracious, barrier-breaking summons of God. Jesus got into trouble for practicing a scandalously open- handed table fellowship, calling the lost and orphaned back home."

Is the person you called drawing you closer into the family of God or are you the family member drawing this person closer to God? Either way, may your conversation lead to something that brings both of you home.

CHALLENGE #12

DONATE FRESH FRUIT TO A LOCAL FOOD PANTRY

#HOLYMISCHIEF

Your challenge: Most food pantries collect non-perishable food because it is easier to store, but some collect fresh food when they have the means to give it away before it spoils. Perishable food is typically healthier yet harder to come by for those in need. Find a local pantry what will take fresh food and donate to them.

LUKE 6 :43-45

A Tree and Its Fruit

43 "No good tree bears bad fruit, nor again does a bad tree bear good fruit; **44** for each tree is known by its own fruit. Figs are not gathered from thorns, nor are grapes picked from a bramble bush. **45** The good person out of the good treasure of the heart produces good, and the evil person out of

*evil treasure produces evil; for it is out of
the abundance of the heart that the mouth
speaks.*

In explaining this scripture, Tertullian once said, "A corrupt tree will never yield good fruit, unless the better nature be grafted into it; nor will a good tree produce evil fruit, except by the same process of cultivation."

Feeding the hungry as a means of grace is not about mindless repetition, but a deepening of the grace that is already happening within us. Once we acknowledge that grace, God calls us to respond in ways that make a difference not only in our life, but also in the world. Donating food to others is not just a good work for us, but an understanding that we still live in a broken world and that we are ready to do all that we can to mend it as agents of God.

CHALLENGE #13

PRAY THE LORD'S PRAYER TWICE TODAY PRAY ALONE AND THEN WITH ANOTHER BELIEVER

#HOLYMISCHIEF
LENTEN CHALLENGE

Your challenge: Pray the prayer found in the following scripture. Notice it is written to be prayed in community. Find another person to pray with today then discuss what that means to each of you. Share your experience on our Facebook group or with a pastor.

MATTHEW 6 :5-15

Concerning Prayer

5 "And whenever you pray, do not be like the hypocrites; for they love to stand and pray in the synagogues and at the street corners, so that they may be seen by others. Truly I tell you, they have received their reward. 6 But whenever you pray, go into your room and shut the door and pray to

your Father who is in secret; and your
Father who sees in secret will reward you.

7 "When you are praying, do not heap up
empty phrases as the Gentiles do; for they
think that they will be heard because of
their many words. **8** Do not be like them,
for your Father knows what you need
before you ask him.

9 "Pray then in this way:
Our Father in heaven,
hallowed be your name.

10

Your kingdom come.
Your will be done,
on earth as it is in heaven.

11

Give us this day our daily bread.

12

And forgive us our debts,
as we also have forgiven our debtors.

13

And do not bring us to the time of trial,
but rescue us from the evil one.

14 For if you forgive others their trespasses,
your heavenly Father will also forgive
you; **15** but if you do not forgive others,
neither will your Father forgive your
trespasses.

Read this prayer in multiple translations in order to hear it in new ways. What did you hear that you have not heard before? If you've never kept a prayer journal, consider starting one. It's brilliant to see how God answers prayer over time.

CHALLENGE #14

SHARE WITH YOUR FAMILY HOW YOU THINK THE WORLD COULD BETTER

#HOLYMISCHIEF
LENTEN CHALLENGE

Your challenge: Spend some time with your family today discussing ways in which the world could be better and how you as a family could change it. To get started, use the following questions:

JOHN 4:1-42

Jesus and the Woman of Samaria

4 Now when Jesus learned that the Pharisees had heard, "Jesus is making and baptizing more disciples than John" 2 —although it was not Jesus himself but his disciples who baptized— 3 he left Judea and started back to Galilee. 4 But he had to go through Samaria. 5 So he came to a Samaritan city called Sychar, near the plot of ground that Jacob had given to his son Joseph. 6 Jacob's

47

well was there, and Jesus, tired out by his journey, was sitting by the well. It was about noon.

7 A Samaritan woman came to draw water, and Jesus said to her, "Give me a drink." **8** (His disciples had gone to the city to buy food.) **9** The Samaritan woman said to him, "How is it that you, a Jew, ask a drink of me, a woman of Samaria?" (Jews do not share things in common with Samaritans.) **10** Jesus answered her, "If you knew the gift of God, and who it is that is saying to you, 'Give me a drink,' you would have asked him, and he would have given you living water." **11** The woman said to him, "Sir, you have no bucket, and the well is deep. Where do you get that living water? **12** Are you greater than our ancestor Jacob, who gave us the well, and with his sons and his flocks drank from it?" **13** Jesus said to her, "Everyone who drinks of this water will be thirsty again, **14** but those who drink of the water that I will give them will never be thirsty. The water that I will give will become in them a spring of water gushing up to eternal life." **15** The woman said to him, "Sir, give me this water, so that I may never be thirsty or have to keep coming here to draw water."

16 Jesus said to her, "Go, call your husband, and come back." **17** The woman answered him, "I have no husband." Jesus said to her, "You are right in saying, 'I have no husband'; *18* for you have had five husbands, and the one you have now is not your husband. What you have said is true!" *19* The woman said to him, "Sir, I see that you are a prophet. *20* Our ancestors worshiped on this mountain, but you say that the place where people must worship is in Jerusalem." *21* Jesus said to her, "Woman, believe me, the hour is coming when you will worship the Father neither on this mountain nor in Jerusalem. *22* You worship what you do not know; we worship what we know, for salvation is from the Jews. *23* But the hour is coming, and is now here, when the true worshipers will worship the Father in spirit and truth, for the Father seeks such as these to worship him. *24* God is spirit, and those who worship him must worship in spirit and truth." *25* The woman said to him, "I know that Messiah is coming" (who is called Christ). "When he comes, he will proclaim all things to us." *26* Jesus said to her, "I am he, the one who is speaking to you."

27 Just then his disciples came. They were astonished that he was speaking with a woman, but no one said, "What do you want?" or, "Why are you speaking with her?" *28* Then the woman left her water jar and went back to the city. She said to the people, **29** "Come and see a man who told me everything I have ever done! He cannot be the Messiah, can he?" **30** They left the city and were on their way to him.

31 Meanwhile the disciples were urging him, "Rabbi, eat something." **32** But he said to them, "I have food to eat that you do not know about." **33** So the disciples said to one another, "Surely no one has brought him something to eat?" **34** Jesus said to them, "My food is to do the will of him who sent me and to complete his work. **35** Do you not say, 'Four months more, then comes the harvest'? But I tell you, look around you, and see how the fields are ripe for harvesting. **36** The reaper is already receiving wages and is gathering fruit for eternal life, so that sower and reaper may rejoice together. **37** For here the saying holds true, 'One sows and another reaps.' **38** I sent you to reap that for which you did not labor. Others have labored, and you have entered into their labor."

39 Many Samaritans from that city believed in him because of the woman's testimony, "He told me everything I have ever done." **40** So when the Samaritans came to him, they asked him to stay with them; and he stayed there two days. **41** And many more believed because of his word. **42** They said to the woman, "It is no

longer because of what you said that we
believe, for we have heard for ourselves,
and we know that this is truly the Savior of
the world."

- Discussion: What is Jesus saying in this text?
- Name a kindness you would describe as an act of love. What other kindness could be described as an act of love?
- Talk about an experience when you realized that God loves you.
- Talk about a time when you did not feel loved.
- What is one of your first memories of being loved?
- What are some loving experiences you have had at church – in Sunday school, worship, on retreat, during a special program?

Complete one of these sentences (or create your own):

- God is with me when…
- A person I know who shares God's love is…
- My favorite story about love in the Bible is…
- I would like to tell stories about Jesus to…
- A favorite memory about church is…
- The best church retreat ever was when…
- If I preached a sermon, it would be about…
- I like to be with my family when we…

CHALLENGE #15

RAINY DAY? SHARE YOUR UMBRELLA WITH SOMEONE WALKING THROUGH A PARKING LOT

#HOLYMISCHIEF
LENTEN CHALLENGE

Your challenge: The next rainy day, walk someone in or out of work, church, the store, etc with an umbrella. Tell them to have a marvelous day, no matter what the weather is like.

MARK 4:35-41

Jesus Stills a Storm

35 On that day, when evening had come, he said to them, "Let us go across to the other side." 36 And leaving the crowd behind, they took him with them in the boat, just as he was. Other boats were with him. 37 A great windstorm arose, and the waves beat into the boat, so that the boat was already being swamped. 38 But he was in the stern, asleep on the cushion; and they woke him up and said to him, "Teacher, do you not care that we are perishing?" **39** *He woke up and rebuked the wind, and said to the sea, "Peace! Be still!" Then the wind ceased, and there was a dead calm.* **40** *He said to them, "Why are you afraid? Have you still no faith?"* **41** *And they were filled with great awe and said to one another, "Who then is this, that even the wind and the sea obey him?"*

In a sermon by Rev. Edward Markquart we hear, "This story for today is an invitation for us to trust God. To trust God not merely when life is good, in the the good times when we have plenty of health, cash and family around. But to trust God in the midst of the storms of life. The disciples did not realize that the power and presence of God was with them during their storm. They could have simply trusted God, trusted that God was with them. In this text, we are invited to trust God, especially during our own personal storms of life."

When we trust God, even when times are bad, we are showing others how powerful God is. We can show people that even on the other side of this storm, we will have peace and we will be transformed.

CHALLENGE #16
GIVE A MINT TO SOMEONE

#HOLYMISCHIEF
LENTEN CHALLENGE

Your challenge: Offer someone a mint today. Make sure you take one too.

LUKE 8:4-8

The Parable of the Sower

4 When a great crowd gathered and people from town after town came to him, he said in a parable: 5 "A sower went out to sow his seed; and as he sowed, some fell on the path and was trampled on, and the birds of the air ate it up. 6 Some fell on the rock; and as it grew up, it withered for lack of moisture. 7 Some fell among thorns, and the thorns grew with it and choked it. 8 Some fell into good soil, and when it grew, it produced a hundredfold." As he

said this, he called out, "Let anyone with
ears to hear listen!"

When we spread the message of Jesus' love, we typically do that face to face. Sure, we might proclaim our faith virtually via email, social media, or text messages, but for someone to truly understand that our faith is deep, they need to see us putting our faith into action. That means we need to be somewhat physically close to others. You have the breath of God within you. Share a mint with someone and know that when you are close to someone, you might be scattering seeds of faith in ways you are unaware of.

CHALLENGE #17

SURPRISE SOMEONE WITH A CELEBRATION JUST BECAUSE THEY ARE AWESOME!

Your challenge: Pick someone in your life to celebrate. It could be a relative that doesn't live with you, a co-worker, a teacher, fellow student, friend or neighbor. Be sure it's not their birthday or other big day to celebrate and surprise them with a celebration. It doesn't have to be big, expensive, or take a lot of time. It can be as simple as writing handwritten notes letting them know that they are amazing or getting balloons and confetti to celebrate. Perhaps surprise that special person with a cupcake or small gift. Invite others to be part of this act of holy mischief and share the fun! Don't forget to take some pictures and share the story on our Facebook group!

MATTHEW 7:12

The Golden Rule
12 "In everything do to others as you would

have them do to you; for this is the law and the prophets.

In 1750 John Wesley said that the Golden Rule is the "royal law, that golden rule of mercy as well as justice, which even the heathen emperor caused to be written over the gate of his palace." While you might not always want a surprise celebration for yourself, everyone wants to feel visible and valued in ways that are appropriate for them. Pay attention and people will show you how they want to be treated. Treat everyone you meet with respect. They are a child of God.

CHALLENGE #18

SHARE SOMETHING YOU KNOW TO BE TRUE
WITH SOMEONE ELSE

#HOLYMISCHIEF
LENTEN CHALLENGE

Your challenge: What do you know to be true? Your faith? Advice? A great quote? Share that with someone today.

JOHN 5:30-47

Witnesses to Jesus

30 *"I can do nothing on my own. As I hear, I judge; and my judgment is just, because I seek to do not my own will but the will of him who sent me.*

31 *"If I testify about myself, my testimony is not true.* **32** *There is another who testifies on my behalf, and I know that his testimony to me is true.* **33** *You sent messengers to John, and he testified to the truth.* **34** *Not that I accept such human testimony, but I say these things so that* *you may be saved.* **35** *He was a burning and shining lamp, and you were willing to rejoice for a while in his light.* **36** *But I have a testimony greater than John's. The works that the Father has given me to complete, the very works that I am doing, testify on my behalf that the Father has sent me.* **37** *And the Father who sent me has himself testified on my behalf. You have never heard his voice or seen his form,* **38** *and you do not have his word abiding in you, because you do not believe him whom he has sent.*

39 *"You search the scriptures because you think that in them you have eternal life; and it is they that testify on my behalf.* **40** *Yet you refuse to come to me to have life.* **41** *I do not accept glory from human beings.* **42** *But I know that you do not have the love of God in you.* **43** *I have come in my Father's name, and you do not accept me; if another comes in his own name, you will accept him.* **44** *How can you believe when you accept glory from one another and do not seek the glory that comes from the one who alone is God?* **45** *Do not think that I will accuse you before the Father; your accuser is Moses, on whom you have set your hope.* **46** *If you believed Moses, you would believe me, for he wrote about me.* **47** *But*

if you do not believe what he wrote, how
will you believe what I say?"

George Washington once said, "Truth will ultimately prevail where there is pains to bring it to light." It is hard to share something we know to be true because truth is not always accepted. As you share your truth today, notice how the other person reacts. Did they agree or accept it? Did they push back? Not everyone agreed with Jesus, but he persisted because he was bringing the truth to light not just in what he said, but also in what he did for us.

CHALLENGE #19
PAY IT BACKWARDS

#HOLY Mischief
LENTEN CHALLENGE

Your challenge: Today pay for the person behind you in line or at the drive through.

MARK 6 :30-44

Feeding the Five Thousand

30 The apostles gathered around Jesus, and told him all that they had done and taught. **31** He said to them, "Come away to a deserted place all by yourselves and rest a while." For many were coming and going, and they had no leisure even to eat. **32** And they went away in the boat to a deserted place by themselves. **33** Now many saw them going and recognized them, and they hurried there on foot from all the towns and arrived ahead of them. *34 As he went ashore, he saw a great crowd; and he had compassion for them, because they were like sheep without a shepherd; and he began to teach them many things. 35 When it grew late, his disciples came to him and said, "This is a deserted place, and the hour is now very late; 36 send them away so that they may go into the surrounding country and villages and buy something for themselves to eat." 37 But he answered them, "You give them something to eat." They said to him, "Are we to go and buy two hundred denarii worth of bread, and give it to them to eat?" 38 And he said to them, "How many loaves have you? Go and see." When they had found out, they said, "Five, and two fish." 39 Then he ordered them to get all the people to sit down in groups on the green grass. 40 So they sat down in groups of hundreds and of fifties. 41 Taking the five loaves and the two fish, he looked up to heaven, and blessed and broke the loaves, and gave them to his disciples to set before the people; and he divided the two fish among them all. 42 And all ate and were filled; 43 and they took up twelve baskets full of broken pieces and of the fish. 44 Those who had eaten the loaves numbered five thousand men.*

On April 19, 2017, at a Starbucks drive through in Bethel Park, Pennsylvania, a single act of kindness started a chain reaction of paying for the order of the car behind them that lasted for hours filling over 160 orders. When a car could not pay for the entire order behind them, the baristas at that location would step in.

Good works and good deeds can spread. People like to be a part of something that might make a difference no matter how small. When the boy offered his 5 loaves and 2 fish, he probably didn't think it could feed that many people, but he was still willing to pass it on. Do something good that others can participate in. Do it because you love God. Do it because you love others. Do it because small acts of random kindness do make a difference. That's what Holy Mischief is all about.

CHALLENGE #20
DONATE OR VOLUNTEER YOUR TIME

#HOLYMISCHIEF
LENTEN CHALLENGE

Your challenge: Volunteer your time in children's ministry or at a local school. You may not have the time to do something long term, but most children's minister or teachers have projects that you can do at home or behind the scenes that will help them out. You can cut our activities to use in the classroom, help to set up a room for the week, be a greeter at the next big event, etc.

LUKE 9:46 -48

True Greatness

46 *An argument arose among them as to which one of them was the greatest.* **47** *But Jesus, aware of their inner thoughts, took a little child and put it by his side,* **48** *and said to them, "Whoever welcomes this child in my name welcomes me, and*

whoever welcomes me welcomes the one
who sent me; for the least among all of you
is the greatest."

This scripture is about children, but it is also about humility. Jesus did not ask us to follow him so that we could be great. He asks us to follow him so that we can welcome those who aren't great in his name. He wants us to welcome people who can offer us nothing in return. Ministering to children has no immediate payoff, but it does reach into eternity. It will make the world better in the future. It guides children towards the heart of God.

CHALLENGE #21

POST INSPIRATIONAL STICKY NOTES AROUND YOUR NEIGHBORHOOD, OFFICE, SCHOOL, ETC.

Your challenge: Write fun messages on sticky notes and put them where others can find them. For ideas on what to write, try the following:

- God loves you and so do I.
- You are loved.
- 1 John 4:7
- Philippians 1:3
- With God all things are possible.
- Smile.
- You are beautiful.

MATTHEW 14:22-33

Jesus Walks on the Water
22 Immediately he made the disciples get into the boat and go on ahead to the other side,

*while he dismissed the crowds. **23** And after he had dismissed the crowds, he went up the mountain by himself to pray. When evening came, he was there alone, **24** but by this time the boat, battered by the waves, was far from the land, for the wind was against them. **25** And early in the morning he came walking toward them on the sea. **26** But when the disciples saw him walking on the sea, they were terrified, saying, "It is a ghost!" And they cried out in fear. **27** But immediately Jesus spoke to them and said, "Take heart, it is I; do not be afraid."*

28 *Peter answered him, "Lord, if it is you, command me to come to you on the water." **29** He said, "Come." So Peter got out of the boat, started walking on the water, and came toward Jesus. **30** But when he noticed the strong wind, he became frightened, and beginning to sink, he cried out, "Lord, save me!" **31** Jesus immediately reached out his hand and caught him, saying to him, "You of little faith, why did you doubt?" **32** When they got into the boat, the wind ceased. **33** And those in the boat worshiped him, saying, "Truly you are the Son of God."*

The title of this section of scripture is "Jesus walks on water." While it truly is a miracle that Jesus walked on water, what is even more astounding is that Peter did it too. Human beings are capable of so much more than we realize. If we focus on who Jesus is, we can do more than we could ever imagine. Inspire someone today to be the person they were created to be and pray that we can realize that God has created us to be more than what the world thinks we were created for.

CHALLENGE #22
SMILE AT FIVE STRANGERS TODAY

#HOLYMISCHIEF
LENTEN CHALLENGE

Your challenge: Intentionally smile at five strangers today.
Notice how they respond.

JOHN 11:38-44

Jesus Raises Lazarus to Life

38 *Then Jesus, again greatly disturbed, came
to the tomb. It was a cave, and a stone was
lying against it.* **39** *Jesus said, "Take away
the stone." Martha, the sister of the dead
man, said to him, "Lord, already there is a
stench because he has been dead four
days."* **40** *Jesus said to her, "Did I not tell
you that if you believed, you would see the
glory of God?"* **41** *So they took away the
stone. And Jesus looked upward and said,
"Father, I thank you for having heard*

me. ***42*** *I knew that you always hear me,*
but I have said this for the sake of the
crowd standing here, so that they may
believe that you sent me." ***43*** *When he had*
said this, he cried with a loud voice,
"Lazarus, come out!" ***44*** *The dead man*
came out, his hands and feet bound with
strips of cloth, and his face wrapped in a
cloth. Jesus said to them, "Unbind him,
and let him go."

We never know what someone is going through. Some people are going through great pain or mourning, but we never know it. We don't always need to, but we do need to treat everyone with compassion. Jesus understood what it was like to have emotional pain. He wept over his friend Lazarus' death. It is okay to not always be happy, but it's not okay to stay without joy. Your smile might not take away someone's pain, but it just might offer the connection that they were missing to give them hope to make it through the day.

CHALLENGE #23

REMOVE THINGS IN YOUR LIFE THAT MIGHT TEMPT YOU ASK SOMEONE TO HOLD YOU ACCOUNTABLE

Your challenge: What tempts you to do something that impedes your spiritual or physical health? Perhaps something distracts you and causes you to spend less time in prayer or reading scripture. Maybe there is a person, website, beverage, etc that you know you should distance yourself from. Make it more difficult to be around that temptation. Tell another person that you'd like for them to hold you accountable. You don't even have to tell them what it is. Knowing that they will ask about it, is one form of accountability.

MARK 9:42-49

Temptations to Sin

42 "*If any of you put a stumbling block before one of these little ones who believe in me, it would be better for you if a great millstone* *were hung around your neck and you were thrown into the sea. **43** If your hand causes you to stumble, cut it off; it is better for you to enter life maimed than to have two hands and to go to hell, to the unquenchable fire. **45** And if your foot causes you to stumble, cut it off; it is better for you to enter life lame than to have two feet and to be thrown into hell. **47** And if your eye causes you to stumble, tear it out; it is better for you to enter the kingdom of God with one eye than to have two eyes and to be thrown into hell, **48** where their worm never dies, and the fire is never quenched.*

49 *"For everyone will be salted with fire.*

We all have temptations. John Wesley said, "As the most dangerous winds may enter at little openings, so the devil never enters more dangerously than by little unobserved incidents, which seem to be nothing, yet insensibly open the heart to great temptations."

Other people see how you deal with temptations. It is part of your witness. We can't be perfect at resisting them, but we can work on our response to them. Part of our faith journey is finding ways to be closer to God, but often it's the little things that keep us from this task. Find ways to resist temptations. If you need help, ask a pastor.

CHALLENGE #24

#HOLYMISCHIEF
LENTEN CHALLENGE

Your challenge: Walk through your city and pray for peace. Pray for its leaders and citizens. Invite someone to join you.

LUKE 10:1-12

The Mission of the Seventy

10 After this the Lord appointed seventy others and sent them on ahead of him in pairs to every town and place where he himself intended to go. 2 He said to them, "The harvest is plentiful, but the laborers are few; therefore ask the Lord of the harvest to send out laborers into his harvest. 3 Go on your way. See, I am sending you out like lambs into the midst of wolves. 4 Carry no purse, no bag, no sandals; and greet no one on the road. 5 Whatever house you enter, first say, 'Peace to this house!' 6 And if anyone is there who shares in peace, your peace will rest on that person; but if not, it will return to you. 7 Remain in the same house, eating and drinking whatever they provide, for the laborer deserves to be paid. Do not move about from house to house. 8 Whenever you enter a town and its people welcome you, eat what is set before you; 9 cure the sick who are there, and say to them, 'The kingdom of God has come near to you.' 10 But whenever you enter a town and they do not welcome you, go out into its streets and say, 11 'Even the dust of your town that clings to our feet, we wipe off in protest against you. Yet know this: the kingdom of God has come near.' 12 I tell you, on that day it will be more tolerable for Sodom than for that town.

Jesus sent seventy-two people out in pairs ahead of where he was about to go. When we first start on our faith journey, we feel amazing! We can't believe how we lasted so long without realizing the love of God was in our lives! Then we start acting as if the love of God is in our lives, but it takes weeks, months, and sometimes years before other people think to ask us what we are doing that brings such joy to our lives. In the meantime, and at all times, prayer is essential. Pray that others can see that God is making a difference in their life. If you keep purposefully trying to experience God each day, eventually people will notice.

CHALLENGE #25

GIVE UP YOUR CELL PHONES DURING A MEAL TODAY AND TALK ABOUT THE SCRIPTURE WITH SOMEONE

#HOLYMISCHIEF
LENTEN CHALLENGE

Your challenge: put your cell phones in a basket during a meal and talk about the following scripture with your family or a friend.

MATTHEW 16 :24-28

The Cross and Self-Denial

24 *Then Jesus told his disciples, "If any want to become my followers, let them deny themselves and take up their cross and follow me.* **25** *For those who want to save their life will lose it, and those who lose their life for my sake will find it.* **26** *For what will it profit them if they gain the whole world but forfeit their life? Or what will they give in return for their life?*

> **27** *"For the Son of Man is to come with his angels in the glory of his Father, and then he will repay everyone for what has been done. **28** Truly I tell you, there are some standing here who will not taste death before they see the Son of Man coming in his kingdom."*

This scripture passage is about self-denial. Our cell phones often keep us focused on ourselves or distract us from being fully present with others. Here are some things to think about as you discuss this passage together:

- What is God saying in this scripture?
- What are some things that you must deny in order to follow Jesus?
- What are some things that feed your soul?
- How is it with your soul today?
- How can you pray for each other?

CHALLENGE #26

HAVE A "MINI-PARADE" FOR ANYONE WHO WALKS THROUGH YOUR DOOR/CUBICLE TODAY

#HOLYMISCHIEF
LENTEN CHALLENGE

Your challenge: Usually we greet people with a "hello" or ask how they are doing, but today, break that pattern and throw some confetti or ring a bell or play a walk-up song. If someone asks why, tell them that you're getting ready for Easter. Perhaps it will spark a conversation.

JOHN 12:12-19

Jesus' Triumphal Entry into Jerusalem

12 *The next day the great crowd that had come to the festival heard that Jesus was coming to Jerusalem.* **13** *So they took branches of palm trees and went out to meet him, shouting,*

"Hosanna!

Blessed is the one who comes in the name of
    the Lord—
  the King of Israel!"

14 Jesus found a young donkey and sat on it;
    as it is written:

15
"Do not be afraid, daughter of Zion.
Look, your king is coming,
  sitting on a donkey's colt!"

16 His disciples did not understand these
    things at first; but when Jesus was glorified,
    then they remembered that these things
    had been written of him and had been
    done to him. **17** So the crowd that had
    been with him when he called Lazarus out
    of the tomb and raised him from the dead
    continued to testify. **18** It was also because
    they heard that he had performed this sign
    that the crowd went to meet him. **19** The
    Pharisees then said to one another, "You
    see, you can do nothing. Look, the world
    has gone after him!"

The Sunday immediately preceding Easter Sunday is Palm
Sunday. Palm Sunday commemorates the entry of Jesus into
Jerusalem and begins the series of observances focusing on the
events of Holy Week. This Sunday is also often referred to as

Passion Sunday, marking the beginning of the passion or suffering of Jesus leading to and including the crucifixion.

Our reading from John is one of the scriptures typically read on this day. Knowing the end of the story, allows us to reflect on the entry into Jerusalem in a different way. If you knew the person who walked through your door was about to suffer within the week, we would treat them differently. Perhaps we should always be more mindful of what Jesus did for us but his suffering on the final days of his life stands in contrast to how he entered the city.

———

CHALLENGE #27

GIVE A STRANGER $20 TODAY SHARE THEIR REACTION

#HOLY MISCHIEF
LENTEN CHALLENGE

Your challenge: Give a stranger $20. You may have to try this one a few times before someone takes it. They may respond with a simple "thank you" or they may tell you a story of how this makes a difference in their life. If you can, share the experience.

MARK 10:17-27

The Rich Man

17 As he was setting out on a journey, a man ran up and knelt before him, and asked him, "Good Teacher, what must I do to inherit eternal life?" 18 Jesus said to him, "Why do you call me good? No one is good but God alone. 19 You know the commandments: 'You shall not murder; You shall not commit adultery; You shall not steal; You shall not bear false witness; You shall not defraud; Honor your father and mother.'" **20** He said to him, "Teacher, I have kept all these since my youth." **21** Jesus, looking at him, loved him and said, "You lack one thing; go, sell what you own, and give the money to the poor, and you will have treasure in heaven; then come, follow me." **22** When he heard this, he was shocked and went away grieving, for he had many possessions.

23 Then Jesus looked around and said to his disciples, "How hard it will be for those who have wealth to enter the kingdom of God!" **24** And the disciples were perplexed at these words. But Jesus said to them again, "Children, how hard it is to enter the kingdom of God! **25** It is easier for a camel to go through the eye of a needle than for someone who is rich to enter the kingdom of God." **26** They were greatly astounded and said to one another, "Then who can be saved?" **27** Jesus looked at them and said, "For mortals it is impossible, but not for God; for God all things are possible."

Clement of Alexandria said, "Perhaps the reason of salvation appearing more difficult to the rich than to poor men, is not single but manifold." There are probably several reasons why salvation is difficult for one who is rich. Our relationship with money should never be greater than our relationship with Jesus; yet, our relationship with money is often complicated. Examine how it feels to give away money to a stranger. How is it different from sharing your faith with a stranger? Which one is easier?

CHALLENGE #28
DELIVER FRESH BAKED BREAD

#HOLYMISCHIEF
LENTEN CHALLENGE

Your challenge: Bake (or buy) some fresh baked bread and deliver it to first responders in your area.

LUKE 11:5-13

Perseverance in Prayer

5 And he said to them, "Suppose one of you has a friend, and you go to him at midnight and say to him, 'Friend, lend me three loaves of bread; 6 for a friend of mine has arrived, and I have nothing to set before him.' 7 And he answers from within, 'Do not bother me; the door has already been locked, and my children are with me in bed; I cannot get up and give you anything.' 8 I tell you, even though he will not get up and give him anything because he is his friend, at least because of his persistence he will get up and give him whatever he needs.

9 "So I say to you, Ask, and it will be given you; search, and you will find; knock, and the door will be opened for you. *10* For everyone who asks receives, and everyone who searches finds, and for everyone who knocks, the door will be opened. *11* Is there anyone among you who, if your child asks for a fish, will give a snake instead of a fish? *12* Or if the child asks for an egg, will give a scorpion? *13* If you then, who are evil, know how to give good gifts to your children, how much more will the heavenly Father give the Holy Spirit to those who ask him!"

What have you asked God for recently? We are lucky to have prayer. We don't have to worry about God being busy. Of course, He's busy but He's omnipotent and cares about us making the smallest contact. A tour guide in Israel once said, "Prayer from here is a local call." The incarnation brought God to dwell among us. The indwelling of the Holy Spirit is God's gift to us. For Christians, prayer is always a local call no matter where we live. God is shaping us through prayer. Pray early and pray often.

CHALLENGE #29

SEND SOMEONE A "EWE" WITH A NICE NOTE IN THE MAIL

#HOLYMISCHIEF
LENTEN CHALLENGE

Your challenge: Seriously, send someone "ewe've got mail." As an alternative, you can draw a "ewe" with the same caption, but if you can swing it, send a stuffed animal.

MATTHEW 18:10-14

The Parable of the Lost Sheep

10 *"Take care that you do not despise one of these little ones; for, I tell you, in heaven their angels continually see the face of my Father in heaven. **12** What do you think? If a shepherd has a hundred sheep, and one of them has gone astray, does he not leave the ninety-nine on the mountains and go in search of the one that went astray? **13** And if he finds it, truly I tell you, he rejoices over it more than over the* *ninety-nine that never went astray. **14** So it is not the will of your Father in heaven that one of these little ones should be lost.*

From John Wesley's journal: Sat 22 Jan 1757, "I called upon one who did run well for several years. But for a considerable time, he had cast off the very form of religion. Yet his heart was not utterly hardened. He determined to set out once more. And since that time, he has been more confirmed in walking suitably to the gospel." At times, we are all lost, but God is always looking for us to return to him.

CHALLENGE #30

PRACTICE LECTIO DIVINA WITH THE SCRIPTURE TODAY

#HOLYMISCHIEF

Your challenge: Traditionally, Lectio Divina has four separate steps: read; meditate; pray; contemplate. The first step is to read a passage of scripture and then reflect upon it. After reflection, pray and contemplate on the Word of God.

JOHN 15:1-7

Jesus the True Vine

15 "I am the true vine, and my Father is the vinegrower. 2 He removes every branch in me that bears no fruit. Every branch that bears fruit he prunes to make it bear more fruit. 3 You have already been cleansed by the word that I have spoken to you. 4 Abide in me as I abide in you. Just as the branch cannot bear fruit by itself unless it abides in the vine, neither can you

unless you abide in me. **5** *I am the vine,
you are the branches. Those who abide in
me and I in them bear much fruit, because
apart from me you can do
nothing.* **6** *Whoever does not abide in me
is thrown away like a branch and withers;
such branches are gathered, thrown into
the fire, and burned.* **7** *If you abide in me,
and my words abide in you, ask for whatever you wish, and it will be done for you.*

- What is this passage saying to you today and to your life?
- Praise God and thank Him for all the blessings in your life. Then ask for Him to intercede for those in need. Lift up specific names if possible.
- Listen to how God is speaking to you. How are you being transformed by God's grace?
- What is God calling you to do?

CHALLENGE #31

WASH WINDOWS OR CLEAN THE TOILETS OF A LOCAL BUSINESS TODAY

#HOLYMISCHIEF
LENTEN CHALLENGE

Your challenge: Go to a local business and ask if you can clean their windows or toilets. You may want to bring your own cleaning supplies.

MARK 10:35-45

The Request of James and John

35 *James and John, the sons of Zebedee, came forward to him and said to him, "Teacher, we want you to do for us whatever we ask of you." **36** And he said to them, "What is it you want me to do for you?" **37** And they said to him, "Grant us to sit, one at your right hand and one at your left, in your glory." **38** But Jesus said to them, "You do not know what you are asking.*

Are you able to drink the cup that I drink, or be baptized with the baptism that I am baptized with?" **39** They replied, "We are able." Then Jesus said to them, "The cup that I drink you will drink; and with the baptism with which I am baptized, you will be baptized; **40** but to sit at my right hand or at my left is not mine to grant, but it is for those for whom it has been prepared."

41 When the ten heard this, they began to be angry with James and John. **42** So Jesus called them and said to them, "You know that among the Gentiles those whom they recognize as their rulers lord it over them, and their great ones are tyrants over them. **43** But it is not so among you; but whoever wishes to become great among you must be your servant, **44** and whoever wishes to be first among you must be slave of all. **45** For the Son of Man came not to be served but to serve, and to give his life a ransom for many."

The Associated Press dubbed Steve Sjogren the "world record holder" of most toilets cleaned by a volunteer. Steve is known to send out teams of people to engage in servant evangelism. As Steve puts it: "The Church has a lot of work to do in this area. We need to get to work by conveying to the culture around us what we are about. It is common that people who aren't a part of a church (perhaps they are a part of the church...) think we are all about raising money. It is almost inconceivable that Jesus' followers would do something altruistic. We need to get to work by serving others in a big way." Go out and serve! It's what Jesus calls us to do.

CHALLENGE #32
INVITE SOMEONE TO A HOLY WEEK SERVICE

#HOLY MISCHIEF
LENTEN CHALLENGE

Your challenge: Be sure to find out the dates and times of your church's Holy Week services. Invite (or bring) a friend.

LUKE 18:31-34

A Third Time Jesus Foretells His Death and Resurrection

31 Then he took the twelve aside and said to them, "See, we are going up to Jerusalem, and everything that is written about the Son of Man by the prophets will be accomplished. **32** For he will be handed over to the Gentiles; and he will be mocked and insulted and spat upon. **33** After they have flogged him, they will kill him, and on the third day he will rise again." **34** But they understood nothing about all these things;

in fact, what he said was hidden from
them, and they did not grasp what was
said.

The idea of inviting people to church can be nerve-wracking. We tend to over think it. How do I bring it up in conversation? What if I come across as judgmental? What if I get rejected? What if I make them uncomfortable? We tend to ask a lot of "what if" questions that focus on the negative side, but what if you reminded yourself of the potential, instead? What if God has been preparing their heart and has been waiting for me to invite them? What if they say yes? What if they're hurting and find healing at church? What if they give their life to Christ, and future generations are changed because of it? Don't overthink it, just do it.

CHALLENGE #33

HUG SOMEONE AND TELL THEM YOU LOVE THEM

#HOLY*MISCHIEF*
LENTEN CHALLENGE

Your challenge: Hug someone that you love and tell them you love them.

MATTHEW 22:34-40

The Greatest Commandment

34 *When the Pharisees heard that he had silenced the Sadducees, they gathered together,* **35** *and one of them, a lawyer, asked him a question to test him.* **36** *"Teacher, which commandment in the law is the greatest?"* **37** *He said to him, "'You shall love the Lord your God with all your heart, and with all your soul, and with all your mind.'* **38** *This is the greatest and first commandment.* **39** *And a second is like it: 'You shall love your*

*neighbor as yourself.' **40** On these two*
commandments hang all the law and the
prophets."

God tells us to do two things: 1) Love God and 2) Love others. Sometimes Holy Mischief is a reminder to us that we often don't say "I love you" to the people in our lives that matter most. This isn't just a challenge for today, it's a challenge for every day.

CHALLENGE #34

WRITE DOWN ALL THE NAMES OF JESUS THAT YOU CAN THINK OF

#HOLYMISCHIEF
LENTEN CHALLENGE

Your challenge: Write (and possibly research) the different names for Jesus. Use these in the future in your prayer time.

JOHN 16 :25-33

Peace for the Disciples

25 *"I have said these things to you in figures of speech. The hour is coming when I will no longer speak to you in figures, but will tell you plainly of the Father.* **26** *On that day you will ask in my name. I do not say to you that I will ask the Father on your behalf;* **27** *for the Father himself loves you, because you have loved me and have believed that I came from God.* **28** *I came from the Father and have come into the* *world; again, I am leaving the world and am going to the Father."*

29 His disciples said, "Yes, now you are speaking plainly, not in any figure of speech! 30 Now we know that you know all things, and do not need to have anyone question you; by this we believe that you came from God." 31 Jesus answered them, "Do you now believe? 32 The hour is coming, indeed it has come, when you will be scattered, each one to his home, and you will leave me alone. Yet I am not alone because the Father is with me. 33 I have said this to you, so that in me you may have peace. In the world you face persecution. But take courage; I have conquered the world!"

We don't always understand Jesus. We can't possibly understand everything about him, but we can still have a relationship with him that grows deeper throughout our lives. One aspect of deepening our relationship with Jesus is to focus on the different meanings of the names of Jesus. By lifting those up in prayer, we can begin to catch a glimpse of the many ways he transforms us by his love.

CHALLENGE #35

PUT A NOTE AT YOUR TABLE OR DESK ASKING HOW YOU CAN PRAY FOR OTHERS

#HOLYMISCHIEF
LENTEN CHALLENGE

Your challenge: Offer to pray for others today. Put a note at your desk or table asking how you can pray for others. When someone tells you how you can pray for them, pause then and pray together.

MARK 11:15-19

Jesus Cleanses the Temple

15 *Then they came to Jerusalem. And he entered the temple and began to drive out those who were selling and those who were buying in the temple, and he overturned the tables of the money changers and the seats of those who sold doves;* **16** *and he would not allow anyone to carry anything through the temple.* **17** *He was teaching and saying, "Is it not written,*

'My house shall be called a house of prayer for
   all the nations'?
But you have made it a den of robbers."
18 And when the chief priests and the scribes
   heard it, they kept looking for a way to kill
   him; for they were afraid of him, because
   the whole crowd was spellbound by his
   teaching. **19** And when evening came,
   Jesus and his disciples went out of the city.

Jesus turned over tables because the temple was not being used as a house of prayer. If you are a temple of the Holy Spirit, you should always be ready to pray for others. Your prayers do not have to use big, theological words. They simply need to be a conversation with God.

CHALLENGE #36

PRAY FOR THE LEADERS OF YOUR CITY OR STATE TODAY SEND THEM A NOTE TELLING THEM YOU DID

#HOLYMISCHIEF
LENTEN CHALLENGE

Your challenge: Pray for the leaders of your city and/or state. A quick search on the internet will show you their names and how to contact them. Let them know you prayed for them.

LUKE 19:41-44

Jesus Weeps over Jerusalem

41 As he came near and saw the city, he wept over it, 42 saying, "If you, even you, had only recognized on this day the things that make for peace! But now they are hidden from your eyes. 43 Indeed, the days will come upon you, when your enemies will set up ramparts around you and surround you, and hem you in on every

> side. **44** *They will crush you to the ground, you and your children within you, and they will not leave within you one stone upon another; because you did not recognize the time of your visitation from God."*

Jesus wept over the city of Jerusalem. He saw what could be and how far the city was from that. He probably weeps over our cities too. John Wesley said, "God does nothing except in response to believing prayer." If we want a better city, we should be praying for the one we've got.

CHALLENGE #37
TELL OTHERS ABOUT YOUR FAITH

#HOLY MISCHIEF
LENTEN CHALLENGE

Your challenge: Tell others about your faith. You may decide you need to tell your faith story to a friend or co-worker, or you may decide you need to write a blog about your faith. You may decide it needs to be emailed to someone. Whatever method you choose, share your faith today.

MATTHEW 26 :31-35

Peter's Denial Foretold
31 *Then Jesus said to them, "You will all*
become deserters because of me this night;
for it is written,
'I will strike the shepherd,
and the sheep of the flock will be scattered.'
32 *But after I am raised up, I will go ahead of*
you to Galilee." **33** *Peter said to him,*
"Though all become deserters because of

*you, I will never desert you." **34** Jesus said to him, "Truly I tell you, this very night, before the cock crows, you will deny me three times." **35** Peter said to him, "Even though I must die with you, I will not deny you." And so said all the disciples.*

Everybody has a story. Each person's journey is a story of their faith that shows God intersecting in their life, often in powerful ways. Every person's story is worth sharing. Many of the testimonies that get shared are often extremes, stories where someone overcomes an addiction or recovers from a huge failure or catastrophic problem by the grace of God. These make great stories. It helps those of us who aren't so bad off, put our more "minor" problems in perspective. These stories give us hope. Hope, however, can be found in many places. Although your story might be less extreme than others, perhaps, someone can find hope that even in the ordinary, something extraordinary can come from it.

CHALLENGE #38

GO ONE DAY WITHOUT SOCIAL MEDIA AND TELEVISION

Your challenge: Put down the cell phone, computer, and remote and focus on God instead.

JOHN 17

Jesus Prays for His Disciples

17 After Jesus had spoken these words, he looked up to heaven and said, "Father, the hour has come; glorify your Son so that the Son may glorify you, 2 since you have given him authority over all people, to give eternal life to all whom you have given him. 3 And this is eternal life, that they may know you, the only true God, and Jesus Christ whom you have sent. 4 I glorified you on earth by finishing the work that you gave me to do. 5 So now, Father, glorify me in your own presence with the glory that I had in your presence before the world existed.

6 "I have made your name known to those whom you gave me from the world. They were yours, and you gave them to me, and they have kept your word. **7** Now they know that everything you have given me is from you; **8** for the words that you gave to me I have given to them, and they have received them and know in truth that I came from you; and they have believed that you sent me. **9** I am asking on their behalf; I am not asking on behalf of the world, but on behalf of those whom you gave me, because they are yours. **10** All mine are yours, and yours are mine; and I have been glorified in them. **11** And now I am no longer in the world, but they are in the world, and I am coming to you. Holy Father, protect them in your name that you have given me, so that they may be one, as we are one. **12** While I was with them, I protected them in your name that you have given me. I guarded them, and not one of them was lost except the one destined to be lost, so that the scripture might be fulfilled. **13** But now I am coming to you, and I speak these things in the world so that they may have my joy made complete in themselves. **14** I have given them your word,

and the world has hated them because
they do not belong to the world, just as I
do not belong to the world. **15** I am not
asking you to take them out of the world,
but I ask you to protect them from the
evil one. **16** They do not belong to the
world, just as I do not belong to the
world. **17** Sanctify them in the truth;
your word is truth. **18** As you have sent
me into the world, so I have sent them
into the world. **19** And for their sakes I
sanctify myself, so that they also may be
sanctified in truth.

20 "I ask not only on behalf of these, but also
on behalf of those who will believe in me
through their word, **21** that they may all be
one. As you, Father, are in me and I am in
you, may they also be in us, so that the
world may believe that you have sent
me. **22** The glory that you have given me I
have given them, so that they may be one,
as we are one, **23** I in them and you in me,
that they may become completely one, so
that the world may know that you have
sent me and have loved them even as you
have loved me. **24** Father, I desire that
those also, whom you have given me, may
be with me where I am, to see my glory,
which you have given me because you
loved me before the foundation of the
world.

25 "Righteous Father, the world does not know

you, but I know you; and these know that
*you have sent me. **26** I made your name*
known to them, and I will make it known,
so that the love with which you have loved
me may be in them, and I in them."

This is the prayer that Jesus prayed for us - those who would come to know him due to the work of the disciples. Pray today for those who will come to know Jesus due to your work. This is important work. It is life changing and it is eternity changing. Focus on it in prayer today.

CHALLENGE #39
PRAY TODAY AT 9:00 AM, 12:00 PM, AND 3:00 PM

#HOLYMISCHIEF
LENTEN CHALLENGE

Your challenge: Set an alarm to go off at each of these times. Say a prayer thanking God for all he has done, is doing, and will do for us.

MARK 15:21-41

The Crucifixion of Jesus

21 *They compelled a passer-by, who was coming in from the country, to carry his cross; it was Simon of Cyrene, the father of Alexander and Rufus.* **22** *Then they brought Jesus to the place called Golgotha (which means the place of a skull).* **23** *And they offered him wine mixed with myrrh; but he did not take it.* **24** *And they crucified him, and divided* his clothes among them, casting lots to decide what each should take. **25** It was nine o'clock in the morning when they crucified him. **26** The inscription of the charge against him read, "The King of the Jews." **27** And with him they crucified two bandits, one on his right and one on his left. **29** Those who passed by derided him, shaking their heads and saying, "Aha! You who would destroy the temple and build it in three days, **30** save yourself, and come down from the cross!" **31** In the same way the chief priests, along with the scribes, were also mocking him among themselves and saying, "He saved others; he cannot save himself. **32** Let the Messiah, the King of Israel, come down from the cross now, so that we may see and believe." Those who were crucified with him also taunted him.

The Death of Jesus

33 When it was noon, darkness came over the whole land until three in the afternoon. **34** At three o'clock Jesus cried out with a loud voice, "Eloi, Eloi, lema sabachthani?" which means, "My God, my God, why have you forsaken me?" **35** When some of the bystanders heard it, they said, "Listen, he is calling for Elijah." **36** And someone ran, filled a sponge with sour wine, put it on a stick, and gave it to him to drink, saying, "Wait, let us see whether Elijah will come to take

him down." **37** Then Jesus gave a loud cry
and breathed his last. **38** And the curtain
of the temple was torn in two, from top to
bottom. **39** Now when the centurion, who
stood facing him, saw that in this way
he breathed his last, he said, "Truly this
man was God's Son!"

40 There were also women looking on from a
distance; among them were Mary Magda-
lene, and Mary the mother of James the
younger and of Joses, and
Salome. **41** These used to follow him and
provided for him when he was in Galilee;
and there were many other women who
had come up with him to Jerusalem.

The Liturgy of the Hours is a rhythm of public or private
prayer designed to weave prayer into the fabric of our day.
While there are set prayers that you could pray to practice
this rhythm of prayer regularly, today focus on these three
hours as they correspond with the scripture we read. How is
God calling you to deepen your experience of prayer?

CHALLENGE #40
SPEND ONE DAY WITHOUT TALKING

#HOLYMISCHIEF
LENTEN CHALLENGE

Your challenge: This challenge maybe the hardest yet. Take a vow of silence for 24 hours. Listen and observe.

LUKE 23:50-56

The Burial of Jesus

50 *Now there was a good and righteous man named Joseph, who, though a member of the council,* **51** *had not agreed to their plan and action. He came from the Jewish town of Arimathea, and he was waiting expectantly for the kingdom of God.* **52** *This man went to Pilate and asked for the body of Jesus.* **53** *Then he took it down, wrapped it in a linen cloth, and laid it in a rock-hewn tomb where no one had ever been laid.* **54** *It was the day*

of Preparation, and the sabbath was begin-
ning. 55 The women who had come with
him from Galilee followed, and they saw
the tomb and how his body was
laid. 56 Then they returned, and prepared
spices and ointments.
On the sabbath they rested according to the
commandment.

———

There is a lot of noise in our world. It is often hard to hear how God is speaking to us. We rarely stop to process all that God has done for us and is doing around us. Cut out your part of the noise for one day. God may be louder than you think.

———

AFTERWORD

You did it!

[Way to go! Great job!]

Did you complete the challenges? I'd love to hear about your experience! Send me an email at skarafanda@gmail.com. You can always find out about the latest ways to get into #Holy-Mischief at www.ShannonKarafanda.com I'm looking forward to connecting with you!

ABOUT THE AUTHOR

Rev Dr Shannon E Karafanda is a renegade Executive Pastor and a professional #HolyMischief Maker. It's always a good day when you can surprise someone with God's love. She currently serves at Peachtree City United Methodist Church in North Georgia and through the John Maxwell Team as a coach, trainer, and speaker.

Shannon also leads an online movement of #HolyMischief makers. The group challenges each other to love neighbors and strangers for no reason other than it's a bit scary and a lot of fun. Not to mention it transforms the world...starting with us.

Shannon did her doctoral research because of a book suggestion given to her over chips and salsa. It was life changing (both the book and the salsa).

She lives with he-who-shall-not-be-named-in-sermons (or in this bio). They have three kids who used to be named but now require a signed release before Shannon can name them or use their likeness. But she does have one very photogenic, crazy, shepherd-mix dog. Her name is Coco. She's pretty adorable. They live in a town that has 90 miles of golf cart paths. It's kinda spectacular.

ALSO BY REV DR SHANNON E KARAFANDA

The Synergy Shift

When the team at Lighthouse United Methodist Church got together to dream about what their new church would be like, they created synergy. But when Lead Pastor Allan Todd passed away suddenly, they were left with a void they weren't sure how to fill. That was until a new pastor, Mark Jordan, was appointed and the congregation was able to grieve and move on. Shannon Karafanda (Lighthouse's Associate Pastor) tells this personal story of a church that learned some funny and touching lessons from two Lead Pastors when the synergy shifted from one to another.

Includes Study Guide for Small Group Discussions

www.ingramcontent.com/pod-product-compliance
Lightning Source LLC
Chambersburg PA
CBHW060540130626
46553CB00002B/841